I'm Now a Grandmother

Jean Dawn Leigh

jadie

Published by
Jadie Books Limited 2009

Copyright © Jean Dawn Leigh 2009

ISBN 978 0 9561356 0 5

Cover illustration by Ian West

Typesetting by Jake Adie

Printed & bound by
York Publishing Services Ltd
64 Hallfield Road
Layerthorpe
York
YO31 7ZQ

This book is sold subject to the condition that it shall not, in any circumstances, be lent, resold, hired out or otherwise circulated without the publisher's prior consent in any form of binding or cover other than that in which it is published and without a similar condition including this condition being imposed on the subsequent purchaser.

For the slightly outdated,
often underrated,
likely overweighted

Other Not Really Titles

I'm Not Really 18 (female edition)
I'm Not Really 18 (male edition)
I'm Not Really 30 (female edition)
I'm Not Really 30 (male edition)
I'm Not Really 40 (female edition)
I'm Not Really 40 (male edition)
I'm Not Really 50 (female edition)
I'm Not Really 50 (male edition)
I'm Not Really 60 (female edition)
I'm Not Really 60 (male edition)
I'm Not Really 70 (female edition)
I'm Not Really 70 (male edition)
I'm Not Really Pregnant
I'm Not Really Getting Married
I'm Not Really Moving House
I'm Not Really Retiring
I'm Not Really a Grandfather
It's Not Really Christmas

Me a Grandmother?

You did say grandmother, didn't you? Yes, that's what I thought you said. Now don't be so ridiculous. I've never heard anything quite so absurd in all my life. Look here, I'm just an ordinary mother who's spent the last, I don't know how many years, bringing up my family. That's all. Probably no different to what you've been doing. And thousands of others, I might add. Seeing them off to school each day to ensure they get a decent education. You know, so that they don't experience difficulties later on when they have to fend for themselves. Not that they're still at school, mind you. My God, it seems like only

Me a Grandmother?

yesterday that they first started in the infants'. And to think they've now gone on to university. Where does the time go? One minute you're breastfeeding, the next they're young adults at uni. Mind you, that was a few years ago now, come to think of it. Really. And all but one of them has settled down with a partner.

Honestly. Can you believe it? And to cap it all the eldest one is breastfeeding her own baby now. *My* baby breastfeeding! It just doesn't bear thinking about, does it? Oh, I see what you mean now. God, I am slow at catching on sometimes. You've decided I must be a grandmother because my eldest daughter has started a family of her own. Mm. I can kind of understand where you're coming from. But, you see, what you don't realize is that in my case it will have to take more than the simple birth of a little diddy grandchild to turn me, instantaneously, into a sad, old, disenfranchised member of society who spends her days huddled around a coal fire with a shawl wrapped about her. An awful lot more, I can tell you. I mean, I really don't look very much different to when I got married myself. It's true. Ok, I suppose I've got a few grey hairs here and there. And perhaps I'd have a little difficulty squeezing into a size ten now. (Or a size fourteen if the truth be known.) But that's not the point, is it? It's all about how you feel, how you approach life. The way you present yourself to others. And let me tell you here and now nobody would believe I was a grandmother if I had it written across my forehead. All right, if I'm not a GM you want to know exactly what I am. What relation I am to the littl'un. Well, please don't ask me. I mean, how would I know? Not something that exactly happens to you every day of the week. Let me see. Ehm, how about, Second Mother. You know, like Second Cousin. All right, it probably isn't as accurate as it should be but

Me a Grandmother?

until someone comes up with something better it will just have to do. There, I don't want to hear another thing about it. Anyway, if that doesn't convince you that I'm not a grandmother, just think about their . . .

Clothes

Well, I've already mentioned the shawls which, and I may be wrong on this, I suspect is a standard issue item once you become a GM. Can't be certain, of course, but it does seem rather too much of a coincidence that they all wear them. I mean, it's not a garment you see in the shops very often, is it? Must

Clothes

be sent out by the social services department once you're known to have qualified. There's probably some sort of central shawl logistics facility (CSLF?) with computer links direct to the birth registry. You never know. So, another good reason why I cannot be considered a grandmother — granddaughter or no granddaughter. Anyway, where was I? Oh yes, clothes. Well, they must wear other non-shawl items but I can't imagine what shape or form they might take. Mm, difficult. Trouble is those shawls cover up so much it's difficult to know what's underneath. And it's rare that you ever see a grandmother out

Clothes

in the high street fashion outlets doing anything but looking. You must have seen them yourself. I've always imagined that they are buying for their daughters. Or granddaughters, even. Well, it would be taxing the imagination somewhat to picture them trying things on for themselves, don't you think?

Never seen them in the dressing rooms. So, the question is, what things do they wear and where on Earth do they buy them? Tricky. Can't come from a fashion outlet because who's ever seen a GM wearing something fashionable? Which begs the question, who is going to spend money on retail rents and wages

Clothes

selling unfashionable clothing? I said it was tricky. Which leaves us with only one option, they must have bought them during another period when whatever they do feature beneath the ubiquitous shawls was actually in fashion. I know, it's difficult to believe but can you come up with a more feasible theory? No? Exactly! Neither can I. So, as Sherlock would have contended, once you've eliminated the obvious, no matter how implausible, what you're left with must be the answer. (All right, but it was something like that.) Which, in our case, means just one thing: they don't buy

Clothes

any. It's got to be the answer. And when you think about it it's kind of obvious really. I mean, why would someone as old as that want to waste their money on something that, well, not to put too fine a point on it, erm, come on, you know what I'm getting at, something that, how shall I put it?, won't exactly be required to provide too many years' service. There, I've said it. And good sense it makes too. There's far too much money wasted these days and if you live to be their age you must have all the worldly wisdom to go with it. So, good luck to them, I say 'cos when I'm a grandmother I'll probably act exactly the

I'm Not Really a Grandmother

Clothes

same. Now, enough of this rambling, I really must go upstairs and get dressed. Can't think what I'll put on though, seems absolutely ages since I bought myself anything new. But, before I do I must tell you about their attitudes towards . . .

Grandchildren

Well, you'd think this would be the area they'd expect to excel at, wouldn't you? Would seem obvious, wouldn't it? Grandmothers and grandchildren should, sort of, go together like, well, like politicians and call girls. Or schoolteachers and holidays. And they should complement each other, even.

You know, get the best out of each other. But they don't seem to, do they? Well, think about it. I mean, let's look at a typical teenager's attitude towards its parents? Yes, parents, not grandparents, we'll get on to them later. So, imagine, for example, when a group of school friends meet up in the high street while, coincidentally, Mother is helping one select a new pair of school shoes. You with me? How many youngsters leap up and down with joy at such a prospect, mm? "Hi guys, quick, over here, you must come and meet Mummy." How many times have you heard that? Not often? Not ever, more likely. And we're talking about

Grandchildren

someone only twenty-odd years past their sell-by date. A mere blink of an eyelid to you and me. So, what do you think their take would be with a forty- or fifty-year deficit? Mm? It doesn't bear thinking about, does it? These two creatures might just as well live on different planets. Not only are granny's opinions several hundred yards wide of the mark, the dear little cherub doesn't have the foggiest idea what she's going on about when she opens her mouth anyway. Not a word of it. And not because she's out of touch with modern fashion trends. Or that she's unable to maintain a meaningful conversation with something in the order of a ninety-five percent hearing disability. No, whilst these factors are an undoubted hindrance they simply pale into insignificance when compared with the blindingly more obvious language difficulties. I'm not kidding. While these two individuals may appear to have experienced identical cultural backgrounds, their vocabularies couldn't be more dissimilar. Even if granny could hear her little princess's pleas (which she can't) it would make sod-all difference. All right, let's try it. "Hey, check it out, Gran." (Response: Gran looks in handbag for cheque book.) "These shoes are so phat, Gran."

(Response: Gran asks shop assistant for slimmer fitting.)
"Keep it real, Gran!"
(Response: Gran insists that man-made materials are totally unacceptable.)
You see where I'm coming from? For God's sake, she might as well be speaking pidgin Mongolian. What makes ordinary relationships

tick simply doesn't apply when it comes to grandparents and grandchildren. Sure, there's a bond of sorts but it's not based on mutual respect. Or a sharing of common interests. Nothing of the sort. There's only one thing they share: a common enemy. Yeah? Make sense? Too right it does and

Grandchildren

another indisputable reason for my inability to qualify. And if my offspring even begin to regard me as anything even approaching a GM I'll see to it they regret it for the rest of their days. Little so 'n' sos. Anyway, enough of grandchildren, what about GMs and their . . .

Holidays?

Yes, believe it or not, they take holidays just the same as you and I. Well, when I say, just the same, I mean they take a break in their normal, everyday schedules to explore pastures anew. Mm, which is about where the similarity ends. And that's why you could be mistaken for thinking

Holidays?

holidays are the exclusive preserve of us youngsters. 'Cos, let's be honest, you're not likely to see any of them in the resorts frequented by the likes of us, are you? And, of course, this does rather make it difficult for normal folk to get an angle on GMs' preferences. But this is where you're lucky because, by taking my responsibilities seriously in preparing for this hypothesis, I have more than adequately researched the subject to suitably enlighten you. And, take my word for it, it wasn't easy. Well, the disguise wasn't too tricky; a few odds and ends from the local charity shop and a resolute stoop whenever I found myself in their company dealt with the necessary infiltration issues. But the real problem came with the terminal boredom. Yes, losing-the-will-to-live boredom, believe me. You see, not only did I have to hang around clogging up the pavement with a couple of dozen of them for half-an-hour or so on a Saturday morning not having a clue what to talk about but I was then expected to endure a four-hour journey on a specially-adapted single-decker during which time we managed to cover no more than 50 miles. Yes, you heard me correctly, 50 miles in four hours! Which, by my reckoning, works out at around 12-and-a-bit miles-an-hour. And I know what you're thinking, why didn't they choose a more road-friendly time to travel. Like when there'd be fewer vehicles on the roads. Avoid all those mind-numbing traffic jams. Well, that wasn't the problem. And neither did we break down and have to call out a road assistance company to fix a blown tyre or top up an overheating rad. No, nothing of the sort. The roads were as clear as a aid worker's conscience and the bus ran like an Olympic athlete. No problems on those counts at all. No. it was the stops. Every twenty minutes.

Holidays?

Like clockwork. Whenever the driver's GPS found itself vaguely in range of a public convenience the brakes switched to auto-mode. And before you could say 'form an orderly queue, please', they'd formed an orderly queue and shuffled themselves loo-wards until each and every one of them had achieved a state of temporary relief sufficient to tide them over until the next GPS diversion. A pattern that defined the shape of the week ahead: arrive at hotel, loo break, supper, loo break, cocoa, loo break, sleep, loo break, more sleep, loo break, and more sleep, loo break, can't sleep, loo break, doze off, loo break, wake up,

Holidays?

loo break, breakfast, loo break, promenade stroll, loo break, lunch, loo break, deckchair, loo break. Loo break loo break, for God's sake. I mean, how can we seriously expect the rainforests to survive this interminable wiping. These are serious quantities of paper we talking about here. And seriously un-recyclable to boot (don't even go there). So, while you and I are soaking up the sun on some far-away tropical destination our merry band of GMs we leave behind are not only clogging up our roads and loos, they're destroying the planet's environment in the process. There should be a law against it,

Holidays?

really. And another thing . . . oops, excuse me a sec, got to pay a visit . . that's better, now where was I? Oh yes, I was meaning to let you in on their habits when it comes to . . .

Driving

Lord forgive us that we ever let them out on the roads in the first place. We have a lot to answer for. You must have seen them out and about. Another total waste of the Earth's diminishing resources, don't you think? Why the motor manufacturers don't see to it that special grandmother-style cars are

Driving

made available I'll never know. They drive around in exactly the same kind of vehicle the rest of us do. An absolute waste. I mean, have you ever, and I mean, ever, seen a GM use any of the windows apart from a six-inch-square section directly in front of her eyes, mm? Of course you haven't. For the simple reason that none of them do. Oh, I don't know why they do it; arthritic necks maybe. Or some kind of hand-to-eye coordination malfunction. Like the steering wheel is going to point in the direction of sight no matter what. Could be. Or whole-body-desperate-for-a-loo-break rigidity. Or some advanced form of degenerative ophthalmic disorder. Who knows? We'll probably never find out but when is a motor manufacturer going to see sense and stop wasting money cutting all that metal out for the windows and then spending money on expensive glass when the old dears won't ever use it? For crying out loud, all they need is a porthole in front of the driver's seat. Wouldn't make an ounce of difference to them. Check it for yourself. The next time you see a GM coming towards you (hopefully on the opposite carriageway) wave your arms vigorously at them like you're a long lost friend and see what response you get. Try it. Or, rather, don't

Driving

bother, because I can tell you now that you'll be met with nothing but a blank stare. No recognition whatsoever. You could swing from a tree waving both arms about wearing only a loincloth but unless you aimed directly for Granny's car bonnet you might just as well be in Timbuktu. How do they continually get away with it, mm? It wouldn't work for the rest of us, would it? And I don't mean when we're just behind the wheel of the car. No, I mean when we're engaged in anything that requires, how can I put it?, well, 180-degree visual surveillance. You'd be surprised, all kinds of things need that sort of attention. Like, erm, well, sport, yes, sport. Well, imagine a hockey player only ever looking in front of her. She'd never manage to hold on to the stick. Or, a policeman directing the traffic. Imagine him standing in the middle of the road just looking in one direction. He'd get run over, wouldn't he? Or a concert pianist. She'd never get to play the low notes or the high notes. Wouldn't be much of a concert. Don't get me wrong though, driving is a serious business and can present problems for the best of us and I don't mind admitting here and now that I can find it a little taxing at times. God, it wasn't many weeks ago

Driving

that some fool parked his car way too far from the kerb and caused me to scrape the nearside of my little runabout from one end to the other. I wasn't too happy about that at all. And then his insurance company had the audacity to suggest that I wasn't taking sufficient care. Damn cheek! Quite unnerved me, I can tell you. In fact, I haven't taken her out of the garage since. Anyway, enough of my woes, we're here to debate the sorry state of our dear old GMs who seem to think they have every right to behave as they like. Well, I say it's a jolly good job they don't indulge in . . .

Sex

Well, I've got to tell you, this is causing me some bother. Really. I mean, think about it, if they're grandmothers they must have . . . how can I put this delicately?, you know, sort of, well, done it sometime or other. Because if they hadn't there wouldn't be any grandchildren for them to be grandmothers to.

Yeah? Not much wrong with my logic, surely. But then, it all gets kind of contradictory 'cos if they actually did do it it would be because they wanted to. And we all know full well that they wouldn't. Because everything points towards the fact that the very thought of the subject positively repulses them.

Sex

We all know that, don't we? Just image your typical GM sitting next to you on the sofa enjoying a bit of casual TV viewing. You know exactly what I'm going to say, don't you? Precisely! The moment anything as innocent as a pair of healthy boobs appears on the screen she's off. Muttering under her breath as she makes a quick exit to the kitchen to put the kettle on. And, God forbid, if there's anything remotely suggestive of actual bodily contact she's reaching for her writing pad threatening to report the irresponsible broadcasting authority to her local MP. Honest. She simply doesn't believe that sort of behaviour should be allowed in a civilised society. So, given that she clearly finds the whole prospect of flesh-derived pleasures abhorrent it would be inconceivable (excuse the pun) to imagine the roles actually reversed with her cavorting beneath the sheets with a member of the opposite sex. (Or same sex, for that matter.) It just doesn't bear thinking about. And another thing while we're at it — isn't the whole matter of procreation sort of dependent on the two parties . . . and I really don't wish to appear unkind here . . . well, getting down to it because they're physically attracted to each other? Mm? Like fancying each other like mad. Not finding it possible to actually make it to the bedroom before ripping each others' clothes off? Well that's how they do it in the films, isn't it? See my point? Without wishing to unduly malign the poor old biddies, who is, seriously, going to willingly want to disrobe them. More likely to want to put more clothes on them. Cover them up a bit more. Keep them warmer, for goodness' sake! Would make more sense, don't you think. So you see, the whole concept of GMs and sexual reproduction is simply a no go area. A non-starter if ever

Sex

there was one. Which does, of course, pose something of a problem. Well, all right, one hell of a bloody predicament. Where on Earth did the little grandchildren's mums and dads come from? Tricky, eh? But not so tricky when you give it some serious thought. And, lucky you, because I've thought long and hard on the subject and may just have hit upon the answer. Really. You ready? It's got to be the storks. No, don't mock, I'm serious. Which generation gave us the stork story in the first place? Exactly! The GMs. It must have been all part of the Good Lord's plan. Well, he's not stupid, is He? He would have twigged the problem He faced with a whole generation of GMs and simply bent the relevant scientific rules to hand over responsibility to the relevant ornithological department who, one must presume, chose to allocate the task to the kindly disposed storks. Job done. Until the exercise could be entrusted to a future, more aesthetically pleasing generation. Well, could you come up with a more plausible explanation? No, I thought not. Anyway, enough of grandchildren, what about GMs and their . . .

Pets?

I mean, why is it that the vast majority of GMs feel socially inadequate if their lives are devoid of canine company. And not just any old pooch. No, it has to be one with white fluffy hair and lowered suspension. You know, those irritating little things with goatee beards and stumpy legs. Okay, perhaps they don't all have exactly the same distillery-favoured breed but they do all plump for one or other of the vertically-challenged varieties. Anything that isn't likely to draw attention to their own waddling shuffle when they go out for walkies. And it looks sort of right, doesn't it?, waddling along in unison. 'Cos, when you think about it, it's what we all do when we select a partner. And that's all our GM friends are doing, after all. Choosing a companion on the basis of their sharing a complementary set of design criteria. Well, can you imagine our GM shuffling through the park with a greyhound tethered to one of those absurd looking stretchy, extending walkie leads? Or worse, trying to hold back some pitweiler cross by its studded leather collar. Be just about as appropriate as an eighteen-stone, beer-bellied, tattoo-laden oaf taking his toy poodle for a stroll down the pub. No, GMs are just as locked into promoting their image as any

Pets?

other archetype. Only difference is, unbeknown to them, they're drawing attention to how utterly ridiculous they look. I mean, let's be totally honest here, there's absolutely nothing wrong with matching your pooch to your own image. If that's what floats your particular doggie boat then go right ahead. Your image, after all, is what you've spent your whole life perfecting so why not supplement it with a like-minded member of the canine community? Sort of strength in numbers you could say. Or an exercise in image promotion. Nothing wrong with that. Except, why would anybody want to draw attention to their having become a grandmother, eh? Not exactly aspirational. Well it's not something you're likely to be proud of, surely. I mean, to the point of walking around accompanied by your own mini, four-legged grandmother look-a-like. Bizarre in the extreme if you ask me. They even fit them out with cute little GM doggie shawls, for goodness' sake. Tartan ones! What are they thinking? Really. But, of course, when you think about it, it's precisely what the grandchildren want in a grandparent, isn't it? Well, look at all their favourite characters:

Pets?

Mickey Mouse, Donald Duck, Big Friendly Giant. Shrek, for God's sake. They all look utterly ridiculous, don't they? So why wouldn't they want their GMs to follow suit? It's why they love them so much. Why they identify with them. In a way, their own personal Disney character they don't have to share with their school mates. Just their siblings. Which, all in all, will help you understand why yours truly simply does not qualify. Young, fit-looking, trendy specimens like me just don't fit the profile. Grandchildren or no grandchildren. Not a lot different, in a way, to my inability to

Pets? | relate to their take on . . .

Hobbies

Don't you think? Grandmothers? Hobbies? The two words don't sit comfortably together, do they? Something sort of innately incongruous about them, mm? So, why is that? Why should GMs be different to the likes of you and me? I mean, most people seem to augment the more mundane sides of their lives

Hobbies

with a pastime of one kind or another. To form a release from the drudge of a demanding career or to provide a means of establishing some sort of character-defining label to an otherwise unremarkable, insignificant existence. It's not really important what constitutes the subject matter somehow and it's not for you or me to criticize. No, if Honey Humdrum can't find inspiration in life beyond her treasured collection of hand-crocheted, pre-Raphaelite tea-cosies then who are we to make fun of her? No, if that's what energizes her artistic proclivities then so be it. Bully for her. Not for Honey to be moping about

Hobbies

the place not knowing what to do with herself. Oh, no, no — at the first signs of tedium, out comes the cosy catalogue and the world instantly becomes a better place. Pure bliss. But what about our poor old GMs? Where do they go to escape the inevitable bouts of terminal ennui, mm? Well, they must need mental stimulation at some time in their lives, surely. After all, in basic physiological terms, they're not that much different to us, are they? Near enough, surely? And believe me, I've thought long and hard on this one. Searched and searched for something remotely resembling a hobby and the best I can come up with is, and I'm being serious here, soap. Yes, that's all I can find. Soap. No, not that sort of soap, the sort that occupies primetime TV throughout civilization as we know it. As far as I'm concerned, they form the only common thread running through the daily lives of the sad GM folk we are here to examine. All right, all right, I'm perfectly aware that ordinary, culturally-superior individuals, of the likes of you and me, also spend considerable periods of our existence preoccupied with the trials and tribulations of these digitally transmitted characters. Of course we do. We wouldn't be

I'm Not Really a Grandmother

Hobbies

normal if we didn't. But that's where the likeness ends. And it's not that our GM has lost the plot. No, she didn't get the plot in the first place. She didn't realize there was a plot to get. As far as she's concerned, the 28-inch CRT in the corner of the front room is some kind of technological-miracle able to provide her with a window on various groups of interminably tedious characters occupying any number of salubriously-challenged locations around the globe. She actually believes it. Empathises with them. Loves them. Hates them. Writes letters to them via the broadcasting media. Really! You can ask

I'm Not Really a Grandmother

them yourself. They'll tell you they receive hundreds of communications addressed to the individuals appearing on their screens each night. You know I'm right, don't you? Okay, well tell me this: what happens if the telly goes on the blink. What's the first thing our GM does after giving it a good seeing to with her right foot? Mm? Well, I'll tell you, she trots over to the front room window, surreptitiously parts the curtains and spends the rest of the day spying on the neighbours. For all she's concerned, these are the very people that might happen to pop up on the telly in a forthcoming episode. Honest!

Hobbies

It's what she does. They all do it. So, you'll appreciate my obvious reluctance not to be mistaken for a GM. How embarrassing would that be? No, I understand these things. Appreciate the finer workings of the broadcasting media. Of course they don't cart all those heavy TV cameras and crew around the country looking for interesting communities to film. I've never heard anything so ridiculous in all my life. I mean how expensive would that be? All those technicians, producers and directors, not to mention the equipment. They'd need a convoy of lorries on the road 24 hours-a-day to move it all around. Well, have *you* seen them on the road? Of course you haven't. Because that's not how they do it. No, they simply contact the people in the towns they wish to feature on the telly and get them to take a bus or train to the studio where they've built a pretty convincing film set to look like it's where they really live. I mean, it's made

Hobbies

out of chipboard, for goodness sake. Or mdf, I don't know. And then it's painted to look like a proper town. That way, the real people from streets like yours and mine get to look as if they're actually living their normal lives. It's obvious. Hmm, you won't fool me that easily. That's for real grandmothers!